IT'S ALL
A BIT

HEATH
ROBINSON

IT'S ALL
A BIT

HEATH
ROBINSON

RE-INVENTING THE FIRST WORLD WAR

LUCINDA GOSLING
IN ASSOCIATION WITH MARY EVANS PICTURE LIBRARY

The
History
Press

Cover illustrations
Front: 'The Kamerad Counter. A New Machine for Counting the Number of German and Austrian Prisoners Taken by Our Allies in Galicia.' (*The Illustrated Sporting and Dramatic News*)
Back: 'An Unrecorded Disaster to the Enemy – An Unfortunate Mishap to a Zeppelin Through Want of Using Proper Caution When Descending.' (*The Illustrated Sporting and Dramatic News*)

First published 2015

The History Press
The Mill, Brimscombe Port
Stroud, Gloucestershire, GL5 2QG
www.thehistorypress.co.uk

British Library Cataloguing in Publication Data.
A catalogue record for this book is available from the British Library.

ISBN 978 0 7509 5594 2

Typesetting and origination by The History Press
Printed in Great Britain

William Heath Robinson

On 20 April 1910, the first in a new series of cartoons was published in the weekly illustrated magazine *The Sketch*. 'Am Tag! Die Deutschen Kommen!' sought to make light of what was a growing paranoia in the British press – the possibility of a German invasion. In retrospect, the series appears remarkably prescient, and in 1910, though it would be more than four years before war was to erupt in Europe, the theme was both timely and topical. Four months earlier, in December 1909, Lord Northcliffe had commissioned the socialist journalist and editor of *The Clarion*, Robert Blatchford, to write a series of ten articles in the *Daily Mail* warning of the coming German menace. Northcliffe had already published a serial called 'The invasion of 1910', written by William Le Quex three years earlier, and several other papers under his control began to pump the British public full of stories that foresaw the potentially disastrous consequences resulting from emergent Prussian aggression. Certainly, Germany's military and naval expansion was a cause for concern, and in less than four years, Blatchford's views would eventually be justified, but in 1910 it all seemed a touch hysterical to a sophisticated magazine such as *The Sketch* and a state of affairs ripe for satire.

William Heath Robinson (1872–1944), the 'Gadget King'.

William Heath Robinson, the man behind 'Am Tag', was one of *The Sketch*'s most popular artists. His imagined 'Incidents of the Coming German Invasion of England' depicted German spies in the most incongruous of locations, posing unnoticed as Graeco-Roman statues in the British Museum – invisible to visitors despite their pickelhaube helmets – or as British excursionists crossing the North Sea equipped with tell-tale boxes of Schnitzel, Schwartz Brod and Lager. The first in the series, 'German Spies in Epping Forest', showed the Teutonic intruders disguised as a ludicrous assortment of birds, trees and woodland animals following the movements of a single, small Boy Scout on an innocent ramble. It was a picture that embodied two elements intrinsic in Heath Robinson's art – the elaborate and extraordinary lengths

'Mr. W. Heath Robinson at work.' Will pictured in *The Strand* magazine in 1918. His photograph accompanied a series of drawings on the theme of 'War-Time Economies'.

undergone to achieve what are ultimately underwhelming and simple objectives, and his own wry and gentle brand of mocking humour. 'Am Tag' encouraged the British to laugh, not only at the ridiculous Germans in their woodland fancy dress, but also at themselves. Perhaps a German invasion was a possibility – one day – but Heath Robinson's visions diluted and dispelled hysteria and replaced it with a calmer perspective: a case of laughter triumphing over fear.

'A most worthy disciple of the modern school of penmen.' *The Raven* by Edgar Allen Poe, illustrated by Heath Robinson in 1900. The influences of art nouveau and wood engraving are apparent in Will's early book-illustration work and the serious subjects the polar opposite to his later humorous drawings.

'Cape Town' from *The Song of the English* by Rudyard Kipling, 1909.

It appeared, however, that the British sense of humour was not shared by the Germans. Heath Robinson would later discover in 1915 that the cartoon had been taken literally when it was reprinted in the German press as an example of 'the alarm we were all supposed to be feeling at their frightfulness'. The correspondent who had sent him the magazine from the front agreed, writing with amused disbelief, 'I don't think Jerry tries to convey to his readers the same meaning as your original idea conveyed … I do believe he thinks that we have all got the wind up.'

When war broke out in August 1914, less than five years after the publication of 'Am Tag', Heath Robinson was firmly established as one of the leading humorous artists of the day, and would find that his work of the next four years would

HE WOULD FALL INTO AN EXTASIE

be unavoidably influenced by what he called 'the all-consuming topic'. The portly German soldiers, relics from the Franco-Prussian War, with their straining tunic buttons and ubiquitous pickelhaube helmets of 1910, became an amusing, if anachronistic, blueprint for the characters that would begin to populate his wartime cartoons, the majority of which were published in *The Sketch*, *The Illustrated Sporting and Dramatic News*, *The Bystander* and, less frequently, *The Strand*. Of editor Bruce Ingram's decision to publish him in *The Sketch* in 1906,

Illustration from *The Works of Rabelais*, published in 1904 and featuring 250 illustrations by Heath Robinson. An ambitious enterprise, it was to be the financial undoing of its publisher Grant Richards.

Heath Robinson admitted it 'fairly launched me on my career as a humorous artist', even though around the same time his pictures had already begun to appear in rival publications *The Tatler* and *The Bystander*. Nonetheless, Heath Robinson would become associated with *The Sketch* more than any other publication, and by January 1911 he was profiled in a series of 'Photographic Interviews' within the magazine. Writing glowingly of 'the famous "Sketch" artist', *The Sketch* declared, 'the work of Mr. Heath Robinson has always been an abiding joy since it first graced these pages with its delightful humour, its unforced yet vivid imagination, and the technical skill of its execution.'

The Sketch, launched in 1893 as a sister to the prestigious *Illustrated London News*, was published each Wednesday and catered to a middle- and upper-class readership, bringing news and gossip on an eclectic mix of subjects to those who enjoyed, or aspired to, a more leisured existence. Alongside coverage of theatre, sport, celebrity, royalty, high society and fashion there was a liberal seasoning of high-quality illustration, most commonly in the form of several full- or double-page humorous drawings featured in each issue. The Edwardian era saw the heyday of the magazine artist, with work aplenty for those who had the talent and ideas to feed what seemed to be an insatiable market. Edgar Rowan, writing of Heath Robinson's meteoric rise in *The Young Man* magazine in March 1908, put the artist's success into context:

> Within the past ten or fifteen years processes for reproducing drawings in journals and magazines have improved so rapidly, and such reproductions have become so effective and so cheap, that the demand for really good illustrations is well ahead of supply … To-day there are literally hundreds of editors asking for good work in 'line' or 'wash' for reproduction, and the young artist with ideas is much sought after. But he *must* be an artist, for the standard insisted upon is a high one …

Heath Robinson was most certainly an artist of ability, as well as one brimming with ideas. *The Sketch* magazine's slogan, 'Art and Actuality', could equally be applied to him, producing as he did pictures beyond the limits of the imagination but deeply rooted in the everyday trials of human existence.

'Bouncing the Beecham' was one of the ideas in Heath Robinson's series 'Little Games for the Holidays', published in *The Sketch* during the summer of 1910. It inspired an authentic, real-life recreation of the pastime by a group of Royal Engineers in Hong Kong.

But humorous art was by no means William Heath Robinson's first choice of career. The shy and diffident man, whose crazy contrivances would eventually earn him the title the 'Gadget King', had in fact nursed early ambitions to be a landscape painter.

William Heath Robinson was born on 31 May 1872 at 25 Ennis Road, Stroud Green in North London. His family would call him Will. Commercial art was in his blood. His father, Thomas Robinson (1838–1902), had trained as a wood engraver, but by the 1870s had become an illustrator of current events for the *Penny Illustrated Paper*, which had begun in 1861. One of Heath Robinson's biographers, Langston Day, describes Thomas Robinson as a 'pillar' of the 'P.I.P.', as the paper was popularly known; it was he who pictured the majority of the leading news events of the day for its 200,000 readers, from the Tay Bridge Disaster to the Maybrick murder. A generation back, Thomas Robinson's own father, another Thomas (1806–85) born in County Durham, was a bookbinder for the pioneering wood engraver Thomas Bewick, and eventually migrated to London, where he became an engraver himself for magazines such as *Good Words* and *The London Journal*. Islington and the surrounding area of North London became a centre for firms of wood engravers (nicknamed 'peckers'), the artistic community growing as the explosion of magazines and newspapers during the second half of the nineteenth century produced a corresponding demand for their services. The younger Thomas Robinson married Eliza Heath, the daughter of an innkeeper, in 1868. Their first child, Thomas, was born in 1869, another son, Charles, in 1870, followed by Will in 1872. The Robinson children would eventually number six in total, with the addition of Mary in 1874, George in 1879 and Florence in 1883. Another daughter, Mabel, died in infancy. Will's father, having elevated his status to 'artist on wood' by the 1870s, moved his family to Benwell Road, near Highbury Fields. Grandfather Robinson, as well as an aunt, lived in the same road, making for a close-knit family life and happy childhood. The boys attended a local dame school and later Will went to Holloway College from 1880 to 1884, followed by Islington Probationary School until 1887, where he found academic success largely eluded him. He was, however, inspired by one schoolmistress who taught

Half-Hours at Eton. — By W. Heath Robinson.

IV.—HAIR - CUTTING DAY.

DRAWN BY W. HEATH ROBINSON.

'Half-Hours at Eton – IV. Hair-cutting Day' from *The Sketch*, 1910. A rare example of efficiency improved by one of Heath Robinson's crazy ideas.

electricity and magnetism, a subject that sparked his interest and would eventually be manifested in his later drawings. At home, among the numerous books the children were encouraged to read, Will took an unhealthy interest in illustrations inside the family's copy of *Foxe's Book of Martyrs* by John Foxe, poring over the grisly collection of torture techniques and agonising demises. In common with many Victorian children of that time, he created his own toy theatres, a pastime that brought together artistry and mechanical function and, again, sowed the seeds of Will's future specialism. Real-life theatre trips, typically to the pantomime at Christmas (once in a box at Drury Lane), were a spell-binding treat. As the boys got older, they delighted in taking rambles, heading northwards up Holloway and Archway Roads to more open countryside. High Barnet was their aim, but they rarely made it further than Finchley before the 'Three Musketeers', as they dubbed themselves, turned back for home. Unsurprisingly in such an artistic family, drawing and creativity were part of everyday life, as Will remembered fondly in his autobiography *My Line of Life*, published in 1938:

In 1918, Heath Robinson travelled abroad for the first time as a war correspondent for the International Feature Service, lending his talents to the American Army. This autobiographical sketch from *My Line of Life* shows him being questioned by a French police officer at St-Nazaire. He narrowly escaped arrest.

We had to be creative, and to use our imaginations continually and at every turn, to make our crude efforts seem real to us. We had no mechanical models of steamships or trains. I think I may attribute the seeds of inspiration for the humorous drawings which I have since attempted to these early efforts to make things out of homely materials originally intended for some wholly different purpose. In such circumstances drawing became a necessity, and a normal means of expression. My father consistently encouraged it.

He was, however, modest about any suggestion that he might have been a prodigy. In an interview in *The Strand* in July 1908 he mulled over his progression towards a career in art:

How did I come to be an artist at all? I can hardly answer, except that my development was gradual only. I suppose, too, the instinct was hereditary. At all events, my father was an artist and my grandfather was an artist. I don't believe I showed any great promise as a boy, although I was certainly fond of drawing, and, like most boys, drawing more from my fancy. I fear I was a poor copyist; in fact, the ordinary school drawing lesson used to bore me as much as some of the other lessons.

It was clear from his underwhelming progress at school that further academic study was not to be Will's destiny. Instead, his parents enrolled him at Islington School of Art, where he embarked on what he called his 'marble stage' of education, so-called because of the seemingly endless amount of classical sculpture he was required to study and draw. 'Nowadays, they tell me, the student is not required to study so much of antique. Otherwise, I should not wonder if artists were sometimes driven to become comic draughtsmen from sheer desperation!' he joked. Will's vision of life as an artist was a romantic one. Those country walks with his brothers had fostered in him a yearning to live as an itinerant artist, roaming foreign lands with his easel as a landscape painter.

Though quiet and modest, his latent talent soon began to emerge while at art school and he was determined to gain entry to the Royal Academy, spending long periods at the British Museum in further study of the Elgin Marbles in order to achieve his ambition. Entry to the Royal Academy, he believed, would be the gateway to becoming a landscape painter. He was admitted, on his second attempt, in 1892.

This photograph of a makeshift shower constructed by enterprising French soldiers at the front appeared in *The Illustrated London News* in November 1915. Significantly, the paper described it 'as ingeniously contrived as one of the caricature machines in Heath Robinson's drawings'.

Towards the end of his studentship in 1896, Will had his first pictures accepted for publication in *Little Folks* and *The Sunday Magazine*, though remained convinced that landscape painting was his vocation. But having sold only one or two of his paintings, and following a discouraging visit to an art dealer in Balls Pond Road who suggested bluntly he pursue an alternative career, Will was aware he could not continue as a penniless art student forever. As his profile in *The Sketch* explained, 'It was that stern mother, Necessity, which compelled him at an early age to give up a systematic art education to earn his own living.' His elder brothers Tom and Charles were already beginning to forge successful careers as illustrators of books; Will decided to follow in their footsteps. He rented a studio in Howland Street, off Tottenham Court Road, with his friend and fellow Royal Academy student Percy Billinghurst (situated over a stables, they later relocated to 115 Gower Street when the smell became overwhelming), and set to work touting his portfolio around the offices of art editors and book publishers, a task he undertook with energy and good humour, likening such forays to battle campaigns.

THE Judges (including, of course, Mr. W. Heath Robinson) are unanimous in declaring that this was the most difficult task they have ever been confronted with, and it was only after innumerable discussions that the following awards were made :—

THE WINNER OF THE THIRD PRIZE

FIRST PRIZE . . . £10 10s.
MR. HENRY BANKES
SECOND PRIZE . . £5 5s.
MISS G. TOBITT
THIRD PRIZE . . £3 3s.
MR. LEONARD MARTIN

In addition to the above a Special Prize of £2 2s. was offered for the best attempt by children under 12 years of age. This goes to MISS DORIS MURRAY GLOVER

By J. W. Ferry

By R. Hervey

By R. V. Collman

THE THREE NEXT BEST EFFORTS

Eventually, his war of attrition began to reap rewards. The year 1897 saw the publication of five books all illustrated by Will: *The Giant Crab and Other Tales from Old India* published by David Nutt; *Don Quixote, Danish Fairy Tales* and *Legends of Hans Andersen* published by Bliss, Sands & Co.; and an edition of *Pilgrim's Progress* from Sands & Co. The following year he illustrated *The Queen's Story Book* and in 1899 *The Talking Thrush and Other Tales from India*. An edition of *Andersen's Fairy Tales* in the same

William Heath Robinson in his studio in 1929.

Opposite: A page from *The Bystander* with printed examples of entrants into the Heath Robinson broadcasting competition. During a radio broadcast in 1923, Will drew and described a picture in which listeners were encouraged to draw their own versions using his guidance.

year was a collaboration between all three of the artist brothers. As leading contributor to a lavish edition of *The Arabian Night's Entertainment*, published by George Newnes, William Heath Robinson was soon firmly established as an illustrator of note. A superb set of drawings to accompany *The Poems of Edgar Allan Poe*, carried out over a period of six months in 1900 for the publisher Edward Bell, sealed his reputation. *The Studio* magazine hailed his work on the Poe volume as 'a most worthy disciple of the modern school of penmen'.

In 1902, Will approached young publisher Grant Richards with an idea for a children's book based on a character called Schnitzel, which he would write as well as illustrate. Schnitzel's name was changed to Lubin, and *The Adventures of Uncle Lubin*, which was published just a few months after the death of his father, exhibited the first examples of the kind of contraptions that were to become Will's trademark. It was also to give him a certain level of financial security. He had become engaged in 1899 to Josephine Latey, the daughter of John Latey, assistant editor of *The Illustrated London News*, and the pair finally married in 1903 when Will felt confident he could support a wife and family. The following year was to see the birth of their first child, Joan; the couple would go on to have four more children, all sons.

During this period, Will had been working predominantly on a series of drawings (100 full page and 100 more vignettes) for *The Works of Rabelais*, contrived by Grant Richards to be a deluxe two-volume edition with gilt and white buckram binding. The cost of producing such an ambitiously expensive book would be a contributing factor to increasing financial difficulties for the publisher, and Grant Richards was declared bankrupt in November 1904. As one of the creditors, Will received just 2/- in the pound.

Grant Richards' financial collapse was to cause Will to look towards the quality weekly illustrated magazines for further work that would promise reasonable and regular remuneration. The 'six-penny weeklies' or 'mid-weeklies', so-named because they were published each Wednesday,

Opposite: Comfortable domesticity is the theme of this 1926 advertisement for Hovis – which could have been inspired by Heath Robinson's own family life.

W. HEATH ROBINSON ON HŌVIS
WHERE THEY DONT EAT HOVIS
THE HOVIS HOME
W. HEATH ROBINSON
HŌVIS
(TRADE MARK)
There is Life in every Loaf
Best Bakers Bake it.

A patent double-action grinder for mashing asbestos fibre

(By courtesy of Turners Asbestos Cement Co.)

A patent double-action grinder for mashing asbestos fibre – a drawing done for Turners Asbestos Cement Co., one of many companies who employed Heath Robinson to bring some imaginative flair to their image.

all featured illustration as a cornerstone of their content. In February 1905, Will's first cartoon was published in *The Bystander* and in the same year a series of cartoons on the theme of love – though of dubious humorous merit – appeared in *The Tatler*. In 1906, Bruce Ingram, editor of *The Sketch*, commissioned him to draw a series entitled 'The Gentle Art of Catching Things', the first of many ideas to delight the magazine's readers over the years.

Will continued to juggle book illustration alongside an increasing number of magazine commissions. He provided illustrations for *Twelfth Night*, Rudyard Kipling's *Song of the English* in 1909, and in 1912 he once again wrote and illustrated another book for children, *Bill the Minder*. But his cartoons in *The Sketch* and other magazines were rapidly gaining him a following and had developed to follow a uniquely individual formula, one where the joke was the drawing itself, rather than a laborious caption to explain the cartoon.

'The humour should lie in the drawing itself,' Will told Marion Hepworth Dixon in an interview in *The Lady's Realm* in 1907, who went on to suggest that he was 'an artist at once so thorough, so conscientious and so original that he can be compared for the moment only with himself'. Contraptions, strange devices and convoluted ideas to achieve often the most seemingly trivial ends were soon becoming the central focus of his work, manifested in series such as 'Half-Hours at Eton' (1910), 'Encyclopaedia of Sport' (1914) and 'Little Games for the Holidays' (1910). Of the latter series, one cartoon picturing a game called Bouncing the Beecham was even re-enacted for real by a group of Royal Engineers stationed in Hong Kong. Their efforts were recorded by camera for posterity and published in *The Sketch* as evidence of how far-reaching Heath Robinson's influence had become.

Will's cartoons were beginning to turn him into a celebrity. In the decade leading up to the war, he was profiled in *The Strand* magazine, *The Studio* (a prestigious art journal), *The Lady's Realm*, *The Young Man* and, naturally, *The Sketch*. He appointed an agent, A.E. Johnson, in 1908 to look after his affairs, and broadened his artistic horizons, both socially and technically, by joining the London Sketch Club, a group of artists and bohemian artistic types who would meet regularly to socialise and draw. He would serve as their president in 1920.

Work for *The Sketch* magazine and other publications may very well have eclipsed his book illustrations in time, but the outbreak of war in 1914 was to force the issue. Tightened purse strings on the part of the book-buying public, paper shortages and increased costs were to see the market for the gift book, which had enjoyed a golden age in the late Victorian and Edwardian era, become seriously reduced. Will illustrated *A Midsummer Night's Dream* in 1914, a particularly fine edition of *The Water Babies* in 1915 and Walter de la Mare's *Peacock Pie* in 1916, all for the publisher Constable, but wartime created a demand for a new type of illustration, and one which Will was easily able to provide. With his 'Am Tag' German characters ready to be revived, he moved quickly to militarise his good ideas.

'The Gentle Art of Excavating – An Improved Dragline Clearing Out the Bottom of the Upper Reaches of the River Thames', from a brochure designed for Ruston-Bucyrus, specialist excavators in the 1930s.

Souvenir postcard showing 'The Gadgets', the house designed by Heath Robinson for display at the Ideal Home Exhibition at Olympia in 1934.

As with many Britons, the war had crept up almost unexpectedly on Will. Since 1908, he had lived with his family in Pinner, Middlesex, and loved nothing more than to spend his free time rambling around the surrounding countryside, accompanied by friends, colleagues and his three brothers Tom, Charles and George. Most walks would usually conclude with a convivial stop at a local hostelry, and so the group revelled in the title of the Federation of Frothfinders, a moniker which might seem equally at home as a title for one of Will's drawings. It was during one such outing in the Chiltern Hills on August Bank Holiday that the Frothfinder ramblers were passed by a military orderly in uniform riding one horse and leading another – 'the first evidence of the war that was immediately to break out'.

For the next four years, magazine illustrators, whether consciously or not, were part of a national propaganda drive. As Will recalled in his autobiography

In 1933, a year before 'The Gadgets' was put on show at Olympia, this cartoon, one from a series entitled 'An Ideal Home', appeared in *The Sketch* showing ideas for coping with congested living arrangements.

My Line of Life, 'I found that already a change was taking place. Publishers were beginning to restrict their enterprise within narrower channels, and these were all connected with the war.' Cartoonists drew inspiration from every conceivable aspect of the conflict but returned again and again to the infinite possibilities of caricaturing the enemy. The Germans might be demonised as brutes and murderers in the imaginations of artists such as Edmund Sullivan or Louis Raemaekers (who Will would meet in 1918), but cartoons that chose to belittle and ridicule could be just as effective. This was Will's strategy: diffusing fear through a heavy application of mockery and farce.

Heath Robinson drawing for television. A shy and modest man, he had no craving for life in the spotlight but was ever professional, ensuring he prepared well for his broadcasts.

Transferring the obsessive complexity of his machine drawings to military training and warfare, Will's German Army used a combination of underhand techniques to carry out their cunning schemes of 'frightfulness'. 'As the war developed,' recalled Will, 'I at last found an opening for my humorous work. The much-advertised frightfulness and efficiency of the German army, and its many terrifying inventions, gave me one of the best opportunities I ever enjoyed.'

One of his first cartoons of the war, under the series heading of 'Kultur', was published in *The Sketch* in November 1914 and showed a small, scrawny gosling leading a synchronised goose-stepping column of German soldiers in training. Kultur was a word used with widespread derision in the British press. Intended to define the best of German culture and civilisation, the aggressive behaviour exhibited by the Germans in the early months of the war, together with such acts of cultural vandalism like the burning of the ancient library at Louvain, seemed instead, to the British, to be the antithesis of 'culture'. Another 'Kultur' cartoon, 'Mine-testing in Cuxhaven', shows an obliging German sailor hurtling down a rickety rollercoaster-type construction into a bathtub in which a mine bobs ominously; a large ruler standing perpendicular to the arrangement waits to assess the heights to which the volunteer will be projected. Kultur, therefore, was a catch-all term, universally understood to reflect senselessness and destruction, whatever the human costs.

Will's comic spin on German perfidy found full expression in 1915 with a series of drawings under the title 'German Breaches of the Hague Convention'. In these, the 'Hun', having completed their comprehensive training schedule in 'Kultur', proceed to pitch themselves against the jovial British Tommies using means so utterly ludicrous, and yet often so prosaic and commonplace, they mine the very marrow of the British sense of humour. Tommies are hindered by magnets that attract away the steel buttons on their braces, or shocked into panic by a sudden dose of unwanted hirsuteness meted out by Tatcho bombs (Tatcho being a contemporary brand of hair restorer). One dastardly plan shows a group of German soldiers suspending gramophones on sticks from which emit an endless dirge of German patriotic songs and

Front cover of 'How to Make the Best of Things', published in 1940, a collaboration with his friend Cecil Hunt pitched with perfect good humour at an audience in the midst of wartime shortages, rationing and air raids.

slogans so devastatingly dull they in fact bore a British sentry to death. On other occasions, laughing gas incapacitates a giggling trench full of Tommies or whittling onions result in floods of tears. It is rare for anyone to be visibly hurt in a Heath Robinson cartoon; at worst the perpetrators are catapulted into an infinite horizon or are flattened, diminished or physically changed, in the manner of Tom and Jerry, only to re-emerge whole again to fight another Heath Robinson battle in another cartoon.

There is uncharacteristic brutality in a cartoon from April 1915, part of the 'Rejected by the Inventions Board' series of ideas. Mindful that the Germans must not always have the upper hand, Will concocted ideas in which the British could counteract German wickedness. The Kitchener Boche-Bayoneter suggested a rickety plane carrying a trench-sized board covered with bayonets, which could be lowered and released on top of a gaggle of unsuspecting German soldiers when released by a snip of scissors from two British airmen performing some audacious mid-air acrobatics. As ferocious in concept as any modern-day weaponry, the picture's slapstick mood and ingenuity awakens a curiosity that oddly dispels any moral outrage we might feel at its gruesomeness.

In fact, the light humour of Will's war cartoons were perfectly pitched to serve wartime tastes. The First World War was unprecedented in scale and devastating in its human cost, with few communities left unaffected by the mounting casualties. Both serving soldiers and civilians at home needed no reminder of the realities of war and so the demand for diversionary humour and light-hearted entertainment correspondingly grew. At the theatre, musical comedies and revues flourished, while in the press, cartoons were more popular than ever. In *The Bystander*, Bruce Bairnsfather's 'Old Bill' was becoming a global phenomenon, while W.K. Haselden, creator of Big and Little Willie (lampooning the Kaiser and Crown Prince), in the *Daily Mirror* and Alfred Leete with Schmidt the Spy in *London Opinion* were all finding a fame amplified due to the war. Of course, the subject could not be avoided, but it was repackaged and, in the case of Heath Robinson, inno-cently subverted. War was no laughing matter, but seen through the prism of the humorist it became a more palatable concept.

William Heath Robinson could easily take his place alongside Bairnsfather *et al.* as one of the nation's favourite cartoonists, with a growing pile of fan letters to prove it. In 1915, his cartoons from *The Sketch* and *The Illustrated Sporting and Dramatic News* were compiled into a single volume published by Duckworth entitled *Some Frightful War Pictures*. A further two collections, *Hunlikely* and *The Saintly Hun*, were published in 1916 and 1917 respectively. It was a chance for admirers of the cartoons to enjoy a concentrated dose of Heath Robinson humour. One letter from the front, dated 6 November 1916, was typical of many he received:

> … Your 'Some Frightful War Pictures' has just reached our mess within the last few days and you can have no idea how much the illustrations are appreciated out here. All members of this mess have been 'at it' since the very beginning and your sketches in the various magazines, &c., have always been a source of great amusement to us.

Soon he was inundated with suggestions for more inventions. One lieutenant colonel wrote to propose that a suitable 'Breaches of the Hague Convention' might be training wasps to sting Highlanders in Flanders. Another idea suggested that enemy troops could be sucked out of their trenches. Both propositions were adapted by Will into published drawings. Many letters came embellished with explanatory diagrams and drawings which gave Will much pleasure:

> … they were all in the spirit of my work, and this brought me very near to the writers. Without exception the letters were written in great good humour by men who were doing their best to make light of their hard life. No greater testimony could there be than these letters of mine to the brave spirit that was abroad amongst our men in France, Salonica, Mesopotamia or wherever they were stationed.

Opposite: Cover of *The Humorist* magazine, May 1939.

AN INTERESTING AND ELEGANT APPARATUS DESIGNED TO OVERCOME ONCE FOR
ALL THE DIFFICULTIES OF CONVEYING GREEN PEAS TO THE MOUTH

Despite ambitions to become a landscape painter, this picture, published in 'Absurdities' in 1934, is typical of the contraption cartoons that were to instead bring him fame.

A Heath Robinson cartoon soon became synonymous with the idea of the convoluted contraption, but his imagining of the war was not restricted to machines alone and sometimes the silliest picture reflected and commented on the silliest of situations. Nothing perhaps sums up the absurdity of war better than his picture of a Swiss shepherd serenely enjoying his pipe amidst tranquil, bucolic surroundings while calmly regarding the military melee in progress just footsteps across the border. Of a similar ilk is 'A Little Frontier Incident' published in *The Sketch* in February 1915, in which a French poodle sits nonchalantly with the tip of its Gallic tail encroaching over the border into German territory, incensing a group of irate Germans. They are a comic reminder of that famous line from Alexander Pope's *The Rape of the Lock*: 'What mighty contests rise from trivial things!'

The Home Front provided equally fruitful inspiration for Will, who, aged 42 in 1914, was too old to enlist and so experienced the war as a civilian. He witnessed air raids over London from the comparative safety of Pinner, and he recorded the constant and very real threat of the aerial menace in cartoons such as 'When the Raider Drops In', suggesting to any families who found an enemy pilot in their back garden to sit on him until help arrived. In 'The Limit', published in *The Bystander* in January 1918, an indignant lady finds herself unexpectedly exposed in her precariously positioned bath tub after a bomb destroys the majority of her house, and a cartoon from 26 August 1914, 'A Nasal Reconnaissance', gently mocks the rampant spy paranoia sweeping the country by showing a group of rotund British police officers attempting to lure a German spy from his flat in Tottenham Court Road by cooking sausages. His series of cartoons in *The Bystander* on the theme of 'Reconstruction' at the end of the war included factory workers laboriously unbullying beef, the Secret Service (in a collection of outlandish disguises) being demobilised and a single, solitary soldier being encouraged towards matrimony by the careful positioning of available fiancées and churches.

In March 1918, the Heath Robinsons moved to Cranleigh in Surrey, where a number of German prisoners of war were interned in a large house nearby. These prisoners were put to work in the fields and Will, who described them as looking 'simple and guileless', employed two men regularly to help out on his land. Although instructed not to feed them, he often accidentally left two mugs of cocoa and some bread and cheese in the garden shed, which would quietly disappear. Demonstrating a characteristic kindness of spirit, he hoped that 'those simple countrymen … found happiness and peace when they returned to their native country and families'. In his mind, the pompous caricatures of German soldiers populating his pictures were nothing more than that – simply caricatures, with little bearing on reality.

Although the majority of his cartoons were published in *The Sketch* and *The Bystander* during this period, other work also appeared in *The Strand*, notably a series entitled 'The Fine Art of Making a War Film' and another called 'When Peace Comes Along'. His pictures also appeared regularly throughout the war in *The Illustrated Sporting and Dramatic News* and, given that the publication was in a larger A3 format and on high-quality paper, the cartoons have a particular impact.

In 1918, at the age of 46, Will went abroad for the first time, selected by an American press syndicate to act as a war correspondent for the International Feature Service, lending his talents to the American Army and, for a time, replacing his usual British Tommies with American Sams. In his memoirs he describes sailing the Channel and seeing the crazily daubed battleships sporting dazzle camouflage and how, on arrival in Paris, all the great buildings, such as the Louvre, were closed and protected by walls of sandbags. There was much more to catch an artist's eye: colourful uniforms of Allied soldiers and, more poignantly, grave markers on the battlefields he visited. Once, he was sketching innocently at St-Nazaire, the main port through which the American Army passed into France, when he was asked to provide papers. He found, to his dismay, that he did not have a permit to sketch on that particular spot and came close to being arrested, though the experience provided excellent anecdotal material for his memoirs.

Opposite: 'Sixth Column Strategy – Stout Patriots Dislodge an Enemy Machine Gun Post from the Dome of St. Paul's', *The Sketch*, 17 July 1940. Probably Heath Robinson's most famous cartoon from the Second World War; he would die before the war drew to a conclusion.

Ever topical, the end of the war prompted Will to draw a number of pictures showing the comic side of

peace celebrations, which took place in July 1919 following the signing of the Treaty of Versailles. He showed Trafalgar Square's monuments clad in armour in preparation for rowdy Peace Night celebrations, and in 'Peace, Perfect Peace' he gives us a street stirring the morning after the night before, strewn with fallen flags and banners, somebody comatose in a postbox and a couple fast asleep on an upturned car, warm under a Union Jack flag with umbrellas up to shelter from the drizzle. Even a police officer has stopped for a doze on a convenient windowsill. It is a charmingly chaotic scene of satisfied disorder, and perhaps an appropriate finale to Will's First World War cartoons.

In the years following the war, comic drawings, the majority of which were published in *The Bystander* magazine under the editorship of A.S. Alberry, kept Will almost continually occupied. Many other titles also featured his work, among them *Nash's Pall Mall* (of which his son Oliver would become art editor), *The Humorist* and *The Strand*. He provided decorations to accompany short stories or poems in the Christmas numbers of *The Illustrated London News* and *The Illustrated Sporting and Dramatic News* ('Holly Leaves'), allowing him to indulge in the decorative style of illustration with which he had first made his mark. He did return to book illustration, but the style of these drawings was a far cry from those he had done for the luxurious gift-book market of pre-war times. Instead, titles such as 'Humours of Golf', 'How to Live in a Flat' and 'How to be a Motorist', which was written by K.R.G. Browne, utilised carefully drawn pen and ink line drawings to lampoon modern living in the very best spirit of Heath Robinson absurdity. The 'How To …' series continued into the Second World War, with Heath Robinson's friend and neighbour Cecil Hunt as author. Their subjects, 'How to Build a New World' and 'How to Run a Communal Home', were ripe with comic possibilities for Will to explore.

Perhaps unsurprisingly, Will's unique style, and seemingly endless flow of ideas, led to much advertising work, particularly from industrial firms who were attracted by his machine drawings. He noted that:

Apparently my strange machinery made a strong appeal to manufacturers and engineers. In spite of their absurdity, these inventions of mine were reputed to be mechanically sound. However, I was always invited to study the real machines and processes before my imagination was allowed to play with them. Indeed, this was necessary, as they had to be at least reminiscent of those they burlesqued.

Thus he found himself carrying out drawings for G. & T. Earle, cement manufacturers; Newton, Chambers & Co. of Sheffield; John Booth & Sons, structural engineers of Bolton; Turners Asbestos Cement Co. and excavator specialists Ruston-Bucyrus Ltd. He illustrated a yearly booklet for Connolly Bros, the well-known curriers, stating, 'I think that I am justified in calling myself an expert in leather'. Ransome's Mowers, Mackintosh Toffees and Hovis bread were three more companies for whom Will designed memorable advertisements. In 1935, when the Great Western Railway cast about to find an original way in which to mark their centenary, engaging Will to produce a series of crazy and crackpot drawings published under the title 'Railway Ribaldry' showed that even train-company pen-pushers had a sense of humour.

A variety of fascinating commissions and activities kept Will's stock high throughout the inter-war years. He was one of a number of artists asked to provide designs for the interior of ocean liner *Empress of Britain*, painting delightful murals on the walls of the ship's Knickerbocker cocktail bar and the Children's Room. He took part in radio broadcasts at the BBC, involving listeners in drawing their own Heath Robinson contraption according to his voiced instructions, and in 1934 a recreation of his ideal home 'The Gadgets' was a star attraction of the Ideal Home Exhibition at Olympia. For the first time the exhibit gave Will a chance to see the public reaction to his work with his own eyes. He observed, 'I had enough of this stimulus in watching the amusement of the crowds of visitors; though I did overhear one earnest visitor condemning it as impracticable.' Despite his success, Will's naturally shy and retiring nature meant it was rare for him to engage directly with his adoring public, and he was delighted to discover what joy his pictures brought to people when he did. Cecil Hunt described Will's appearance at a *Sunday Times* book exhibition, around the time of the publication of *My Line of Life*, saying he was 'deeply moved by the insistence of crowds who surrounded him, not for the superficial autograph, but to thank him for his refreshing humour and the unforgettableness of many of his finest absurdities'.

With the coming of war again in 1939, *The Sketch* engaged him once more to provide full-page cartoons to satirise unfolding events and pitch mirth against fear. Will's Second World War cartoons are even more convoluted and complex, and while most concentrate on the Home Front, there is also the introduction of real characters into his pictures. Two decades earlier, the only real personality to appear in his First World War cartoons was the Kaiser ~ and then he was an unseen inhabitant of a car with a bath tub ~ but Will's Second World War cartoons featured Goering and Churchill, and there were even rumours that William Heath Robinson was one of the names on the Gestapo Arrest List. He was in good company. The list also included the cartoonist David Low, Vera Brittain and Noel Coward.

William Heath Robinson died on 13 September 1944 at his home, 25 Southwood Avenue, Highgate. He had been suffering increasingly from a heart condition that prevented him from taking part in any activity other than reading and drawing. Due to return to hospital for a prostate operation, he was rigged up to a variety of tubes and drips, which he removed when left alone for a few minutes, dying a short time afterwards.

His obituary in *The Times* the following day paid tribute to an artist of boundless imagination and exacting skill, describing him as possessing 'a special genius [that] lay in discovering and exploiting a form of incongruity; singularly relevant to the age in which he lived'. Readers were also reminded that he had the singular honour of being the only artist to be listed in the *Oxford English Dictionary* as the root of an adjective:

He was the originator of a type of pictorial joke so distinctive and individual that his name had come to be used adjectivally. Wherever English is spoken 'a Heath Robinson contraption' is understood to mean a piece of apparatus or machinery of such ludicrous elaboration, so old-fashioned, and so obviously home made as to be an object of mirth.

There seems to be manifestly something of Heath Robinson himself in each of his drawings. Some years earlier, H.G. Wells, a great admirer of the artist, wrote to a friend of Will's saying, 'I don't count Heath Robinson as a human being, more of a joy in life, like early crocuses, watching gulls fly, well-behaved cats, or geese, or a windy common'. As an artist, he obviously gained much happiness from bringing joy to others. Despite the shambolic ideas emerging from his imagination, the neat, ordered and absorbed precision in which they were executed exude an odd sense of satisfaction. His machines may have been a rickety confusion of wheels, cogs and pulleys, yet, miraculously, they work, bringing order to chaos in the most circuitous way. A Heath Robinson picture gives the same pointless fulfilment gained by finishing a 5,000-piece jigsaw or a particularly difficult quadratic equation. We laugh at the ridiculous and puzzle at the difficulty and eccentricity, but we also find a certain peace in the completeness of thought represented in each illustration.

The Heath Robinson cartoons gathered in this volume are taken from the First World War issues of *The Sketch*, *The Illustrated Sporting and Dramatic News* and *The Bystander*, all part of the archives of *The Illustrated London News* housed and managed at Mary Evans Picture Library. In addition, there is a selection from *The Strand* magazine, a run of which is owned by the library. The book brings together cartoons that were to gain Will worldwide renown, and were to soothe the nerves and raise the spirits of a nation at war which found that joy and laughter were the best of tonics in the most difficult of times. I have no doubt readers today will enjoy these pictures as much as the millions who admired and appreciated the art of the so-called 'Gadget King' a century ago.

PRE-WAR PREDICTIONS – 'AM TAG' IMAGES

'Am Tag! Die Deutsche Kommen (Very)! Incidents of the Coming German Invasion of England. I. German Spies in Epping Forest.' (*The Sketch*, 20 April 1910)

'Am Tag! Die Deutsche Kommen (Very)! Incidents of the Coming German Invasion of England. II. With the Aid of an Ingenious Device, the Germans Send English Dispatches Astray.' (*The Sketch*, 27 April, 1910)

'Am Tag! Die Deutsche Kommen (Very)! Incidents of the Coming German Invasion of England. III. German Officers Endeavouring to Enter an Englishman's Home in Disguise.' (*The Sketch*, 4 May 1910)

'Am Tag! Die Deutschen Kommen! Incidents of the Coming German Invasion of England. IV. A Masked Raid on Yarmouth Beach.' (*The Sketch*, 11 May 1910)

'Am Tag! Die Deutschen Kommen! Incidents of the Coming German Invasion of England. V. German Troops, Disguised as British Excursionists, Crossing the North Sea.' (*The Sketch*, 18 May 1910)

The Day: the Germans Come — and are "Terror"-ised.

INCIDENTS OF THE COMING GERMAN INVASION OF ENGLAND — FROM THE BRITISH SIDE.

THE HOISTING OF THE HOSTAGE: SILENCING A GERMAN GUN ON THE HEIGHTS OF PONTYPRIDD.

Drawn by W. Heath Robinson.

'The Day: The Germans Come – and are "Terror"-ised. Incidents of the Coming German Invasion of England – from the British Side. The Hoisting of the Hostage: Silencing a German Gun on the Heights of Pontypridd.' (*The Sketch*, 22 June 1910)

The Day: the Germans Come — and are "Terror"-ised.

INCIDENTS OF THE COMING GERMAN INVASION OF ENGLAND — FROM THE BRITISH SIDE.

UH-LAND! CAPTURING UHLANS IN THE WESTMINSTER BRIDGE ROAD, WITH THE KIND CO-OPERATION OF THE SPIKED HELMETS OF THE FOE.

DRAWN BY W. HEATH ROBINSON.

'The Day: The Germans Come – and are "Terror"-ised. Incidents of the Coming German Invasion of England – from the British Side. Uh-land! Capturing Uhlans in the Westminster Bridge Road, with the Kind Co-operation of the Spiked Helmets of the Foe.' (*The Sketch*, 22 June 1910)

'The Day: The Germans Come – and are "Terror"-ised. Incidents of the Coming German Invasion of England – from the British Side. Gather ye Lilies While ye May: Disguised Territorials in the German Camp at the Welsh Harp, Hendon.' (*The Sketch*, 22 June 1910)

'The Day: The Germans Come – and are "Terror"-ised. Incidents of the Coming German Invasion of England – from the British Side. Weight and Do Not See: Territorials Eluding the Vigilance of German Sentries on the Wastes of Wimbledon Common.' (*The Sketch*, 22 June 1910)

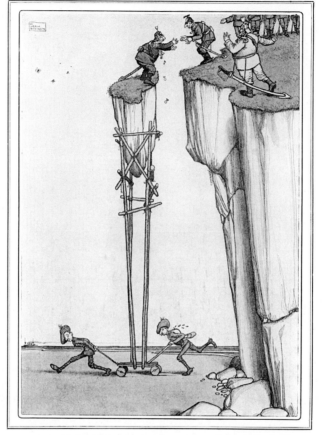

'The Day: the Germans Come – and are "Terror"-ised. Incidents of the Coming German Invasion of England – from the British Side. "Farewell, a Long Farewell, to all our Greatness": A German Officer is Removed from the Sphere of Action on a Detachable Cliff-edge Near Hove.' (*The Sketch*, 22 June 1910)

THE WAR IMAGES

'A Nasal Reconnaissance. Discovering German Spies in Tottenham Court Road.' (*The Sketch*, 26 August 1914)

'Kultur – The New Reconnoitring Mortar.' (*The Sketch*, 28 October 1914)

'Kultur – Mine-Testing in Cuxhaven.' (*The Sketch*, 11 November 1914)

'Kultur – A First Lesson in the Goose Step.' (*The Sketch*, 25 November 1914)

THE KAISER ENJOYING A MORNING TUB IN HIS NEW CAMPAIGNING CAR.

Drawn by W. Heath Robinson.

'Kultur – The Kaiser Enjoying a Morning Tub in his New Campaigning Car.' (*The Sketch*, 9 December 1914)

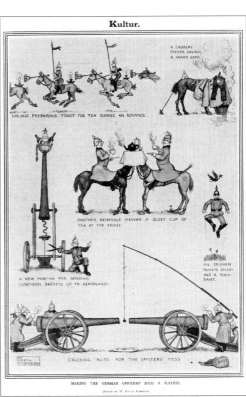

'Kultur – The Drilling-Machine for Military Beginners.'
(*The Sketch*, 30 December 1914)

'Kultur – Making the German Officers' Mess a Success.'
(*The Sketch*, 6 January 1915)

'A Swiss Shepherd Watching a Battle by the Frontier.' (*The Illustrated Sporting and Dramatic News*, 16 January 1915)

'We May Publish This Now! Just Before the Battles, Mother! A Little Frontier Incident.'
(*The Sketch*, 3 February 1915)

'A Daring Frontal Attack on a Bomb-Dropper.' (*The Illustrated Sporting and Dramatic News*, 18 February 1915)

Opposite: 'Recommended to the War Office (Reply Awaited): Patent Applied For: The New Lancing-Wheel for Teaching Young Lancers to Lance.' (*The Sketch*, 3 March 1915)

THE GERMAN PERISCOPER: Ach, Himmel! Dot most be der peautiful Ben Nevis of vich ve 'ave 'eard so mooch.

DRAWN BY W. HEATH ROBINSON.

'Off the Coast of Scotland.' 'The German Periscoper: Ach, Himmel! Dot Most be der Peautiful Ben Nevis of Vich ve 'Ave 'Eard So Mooch.' (*The Sketch*, 17 March 1915)

'Thoroughness. Mopping-Up Floods in Belgium: The New German Method.' Spiking the water with a combination of sausages, sauerkraut and lager, legions of German soldiers manage to mop up floods in Belgium simply by drinking the water. (*The Sketch*, 24 March 1915)

'Periscopomania. The Special Constable (Who Has Strayed into Highgate Ponds): Good Heavens! There's a Periscope!' A serious situation – the prevalence of U-boats striking at British ships – reduced, in typically Heath Robinson fashion, to a very local and laughable hysteria. (*The Sketch*, 31 March 1915)

'A Clever Ruse By Which Two German Officers Carried a Gun Past the German Lines.' (*The Illustrated Sporting and Dramatic News*, 3 April 1915)

'Patent Applied For – The Kitchener Boche-Bayoneter – An Airy Invention.' This rather gruesome invention was also known as the 'trench-presser'. (*The Sketch*, 28 April 1915)

'Picking the Pickelhaube – An Example of British Frightfulness.' (*The Illustrated Sporting and Dramatic News*, 8 May 1915)

'Before the Internments – German Spies Training a Young Carrier-Pigeon in a London Boarding-House.' By late September, 13,600 Germans and Austrians were in internment camps, a result of the hastily passed Aliens Restriction Act, which prevented enemy aliens leaving Britain after 10 August. Spy hysteria was rife, however, a theme played upon in this cartoon. (*The Sketch*, 19 May 1915)

'German Breaches of the Hague Convention I. The Germans Use Button-Magnets. A new method of German frightfulness is reported, in the shape of button-magnets, designed to render our troops uncomfortable before an attack in force.' (*The Sketch*, 16 June 1915)

'German Breaches of the Hague Convention II. Gott Strafe-ing the British by Draughting Them Stiff Necks.' (*The Sketch*, 23 June 1915)

'German Breaches of the Hague Convention III. Shepherding Flu Germs into the British Trenches.' (*The Sketch*, 30 June 1915)

'German Breaches of the Hague Convention IV. The Enemy Trying Their Tommy-Scalders, With Indifferent Result.' (*The Sketch*, 7 July 1915)

'German Breaches of the Hague Convention V. Boring a British Sentry to Death in the Most Inhumane Manner.' (*The Sketch*, 14 July 1915)

'German Breaches of the Hague Convention VI. Injecting Chilblain Serum into the Feet of the British.' (*The Sketch*, 21 July 1915)

'Teasing Tirpitz or Luring a 'U' Boat to Dover.' The Tirpitz in question was Admiral Alfred von Tirpitz (1849–1930), commander of the Imperial German Navy and a strong advocate of unrestricted submarine warfare. (*The Illustrated Sporting and Dramatic News*, 31 July 1915)

'German Breaches of the Hague Convention VII. Tatchoing the British to their Entanglement.'
'Tatcho' was a well-known hair restorer! (*The Sketch*, 4 August 1915)

'German Breaches of the Hague Convention VIII. Lachrymosing the British by Onion-Whittling Under Cover of Night.' (*The Sketch*, 11 August 1915)

'German Breaches of the Hague Convention IX. Laughing Gassing the British Before an Advance in Close Formation.' (*The Sketch*, 18 August 1915)

'German Breaches of the Hague Convention X. Reducing the British Army by Anti-Fatting a Tributary of the Marne.' (*The Sketch*, 25 August 1915)

'German Breaches of the Hague Convention XI. A Grouse-as-Usual Outrage by a German Officer.' (*The Sketch*, 1 September 1915)

'German Breaches of the Hague Convention XII. Gin-and-Bittering the Wells in German South West Africa to Induce Ration-Proof Hunger.' (*The Sketch*, 8 September 1915)

'The Outflanking Machine for Turning Movements.' (*Some Frightful War Pictures*, 1915)

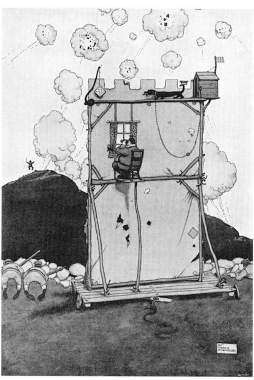

'A Trained Dog of War Drawing the Enemy Fire.' (*Some Frightful War Pictures*, 1915)

'The Enemy in Our Midst! An Extra Special Constable Discovering a German Waiter in the Act of Laying the Foundation of a Concrete Gun-Bed.' (*Some Frightful War Pictures*, 1915)

The Fine Art of Making a War-Film.

By W. HEATH ROBINSON.

Do not pass over these entertaining pictures with a casual glance. Each one contains a number of ingenious and amusing details, sufficient to furnish forth an ordinary number of a comic paper in themselves.

THE FALL OF PRZEMYSL.

'The Fine Art of Making a War-Film – The Fall of Przemysl.' The fortress town of Przemysl in Eastern Galicia was the scene of the longest siege during the war. The Austro-Hungarian garrison surrendered on 22 March 1915 after 133 days. (*The Strand*, October 1915)

PREPARING THE POPULAR FILM OF A TAUBE SOARING OVER RHEIMS
CATHEDRAL.

THE ARRIVAL OF GERMAN PRISONERS AT MARGATE JETTY BY THE
NIGHT BOAT FROM BOULOGNE.

'The Fine Art of Making a War-Film – Preparing the Popular Film of a Taube Soaring Over Rheims Cathedral.' The bombing of Reims Cathedral by the Germans in September 1914 was widely condemned as the new height of barbarism. (*The Strand*, October 1915)

'The Fine Art of Making a War-Film – The Arrival of German Prisoners at Margate Jetty by the Night Boat from Boulogne.' (*The Strand*, October 1915)

FILMING "THE QUEEN OF THE HAREM." A PATHETIC INCIDENT AT
THE TAKING OF CONSTANTINOPLE.

'The Fine Art of Making a War-Film – Filming "The Queen of the Harem". A Pathetic
Incident at the Taking of Constantinople.' (*The Strand*, October 1915)

A ZEPPELIN RAID ON A POULTRY FARM IN THE VOSGES DISTRICT.

GERMAN SUBMARINE SINKING PLEASURE-BOAT OFF BRIGHTON.

'The Fine Art of Making a War-Film – A Zeppelin Raid on a Poultry Farm in the Vosges District.' (*The Strand*, October 1915)

'The Fine Art of Making a War-Film – German Submarine Sinking Pleasure-Boat Off Brighton.' (*The Strand*, October 1915)

'How the Last German Got Back Across the Yser.' In 1914, the German 'Race to the Sea' was halted at the Battle of Yser. The river was deliberately flooded between Nieuwpoort and Diksmuide to provide an obstacle to the advancing German Army, with the result that the area of Western Belgium remained unoccupied. (*The Illustrated Sporting and Dramatic News*, 30 October 1915)

'Rejected by the Inventions Board I. The Armoured Bayonet-Curler – For Rendering Useless the Sentry's *Arme Blanche*.' (*The Sketch*, 1 December 1915)

'Rejected by the Inventions Board II. The Blow-Bomb: A Device for Extinguishing the Fuses of Falling Zeppelin Bombs.' (*The Sketch*, 8 December 1915)

'Rejected by the Inventions Board III. A Device for Screw Stoppering the Enemy's Rifles.' (*The Sketch*, December 1915)

'Rejected by the Inventions Board IV. The Barb-Drawer: For Extracting Barbs from Enemy Wire Entanglements.' (*The Sketch*, December 1915)

'Germans Training Wasps to Sting Highlanders' Legs.' One of several cartoons based on ideas sent to Heath Robinson by serving soldiers. This particular suggestion came from a lieutenant colonel. (*The Illustrated Sporting and Dramatic News*, 11 December 1915)

'Mine and Countermine.' (*The Illustrated Sporting and Dramatic News*, 25 December 1915)

'Rejected by the Inventions Board V. The Water-Bottle Rotary for Warming the Legs of Scottish Soldiers After a Night in the Trenches.' (*The Sketch*, 29 December 1915)

The subzeppmarinellin for making sure of your enemy

'The Subzeppmarinellin for Making Sure of Your Enemy.' (*c.*1916, drawing reproduced in *My Line of Life*)

'Rejected by the Inventions Board VII. The Gallipoli Shell-Diverter for Returning the Enemy's Fire.' (*The Sketch*, 12 January 1916)

'Rejected by the Inventions Board VIII. The Harley-Scope Mine-Detector.' (*The Sketch*, 19 January 1916)

'Terrible Revelation of British Frivolity During a Raid on the East Coast.' (*The Illustrated Sporting and Dramatic News*, 23 January 1916)

'Rejected by the Inventions Board IX. The Pilsener-Pump for Tapping the Enemy's Beer.' (*The Sketch*, 26 January 1916)

'At the School for Strafing! At Count Zeppelin's Evening Classes for Bomb-Droppers.' (*The Sketch*, 1 March 1916)

'An Unrecorded Disaster to the Enemy – An Unfortunate Mishap to a Zeppelin Through Want of Using Proper Caution When Descending.' (*The Illustrated Sporting and Dramatic News*, 18 March 1916)

'Flying Enemy Aviator (beginning to realise): "Himmel! Surely I the zone of fire approaching be".' (Date unknown, original artwork)

'Loot.' (*The Illustrated Sporting and Dramatic News*, 17 June 1916)

'Periscoped in the North Sea. An Unfortunate Experience of a U-boat Through Coming to the Surface Too Suddenly.' (*The Illustrated Sporting and Dramatic News*, 12 August 1916)

'The Kamerad Counter. A New Machine for Counting the Number of German and Austrian Prisoners Taken by Our Allies in Galicia.' Surrendering German soldiers would usually cry 'Kamerad' as a signal to their would-be captors. (*The Illustrated Sporting and Dramatic News*, 2 September 1916)

'Submerged – In an Untersee Realschule: Training a Young U-boat Pirate to Remain Under Water for Long Periods.' (*The Sketch*, 17 January 1917)

'A Pick Nick Down Under – A Sharp Thrill in the Antipodes: One of the Dangers of Very Deep Mining.' (*The Sketch*, 31 January 1917)

When Peace Comes Along.

By W. HEATH ROBINSON.

USING UP THE OLD WAR TANKS AS MOTOR BUSES.

A LAST USE FOR THE OLD SIEGE HOWITZERS.

'When Peace Comes Along – Using Up the Old War Tanks as Motor Buses.' Many London motor buses were requisitioned for army use at the front. Here, roles are reversed. Tanks were toured around Britain to encourage people to invest in war bonds and as trophies at the war's end. (*The Strand*, February 1917)

'When Peace Comes Along – A Last Use for the Old Siege Howitzers.' (*The Strand*, February 1917)

A KINDER USE FOR SUBMARINE MINES.
HELPING ELDERLY PEOPLE TO MOUNT THE STAIRS.

'When Peace Comes Along – A Kinder Use for Submarine Mines. Helping Elderly People to Mount the Stairs.' (*The Strand*, February 1917)

THE PEACEFUL CONVERSION OF A TORPEDO TO A FOOT-WARMER.

'When Peace Comes Along – The Peaceful Conversion of a Torpedo to a Foot-Warmer.'
(*The Strand*, February 1917)

OLD WAR BALLOONS FOR DRAWING CORKS AT BIRTHDAY PARTIES.

'When Peace Comes Along – Old War Balloons for Drawing Corks at Birthday Parties.'
(*The Strand*, February 1917)

DEEP - SEA SWIMMING.

AN OLD, WORN-OUT SUBMARINE AS AN AID TO BEGINNERS.

'When Peace Comes Along – Deep-Sea Swimming. An Old, Worn-Out Submarine as an Aid to Beginners.' (*The Strand*, February 1917)

'A Tale of Two Tanks.' (*The Illustrated Sporting and Dramatic News*, 10 February 1917)

'Self-Help in War Time – Building a Bungalow I – The First Stage of Building a Bungalow – Naturally, Begin with the Chimney.' (*The Sketch*, 14 February 1917)

'Self-Help in War Time – Building a Bungalow II – After Placing the Chimney in Position, the Next Step is to Fix Up the Spare Bedroom – and Don't Forget to Whitewash the Music Room Ceiling.' (*The Sketch*, 21 February 1917)

'Self-Help in War Time – Building a Bungalow III – Now, Having Made a Good Start with Your Music Room, Place Your Piano in Position.' (*The Sketch*, 28 February 1917)

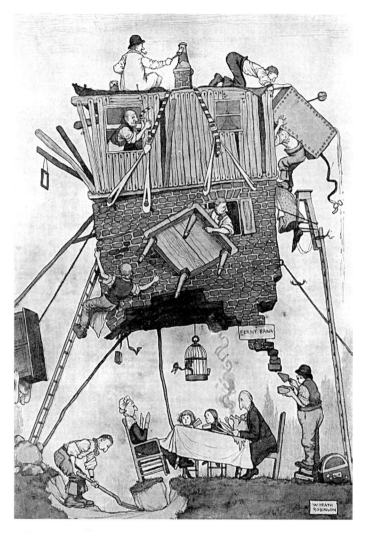

'Self-Help in War Time – Building a Bungalow IV – The Dining Room Being at Last Well Under Way, and the Cistern Almost Fixed Up, You May Now Move In, and Let Nothing Hinder the Workmen from Proceeding at Once with the Foundations.' (*The Sketch*, 7 March 1917)

'All That was Taxed was His Ingenuity – An Intelligent Young Pup Disguised as a Parakeet to Avoid the Increased Licence Duty' (raised on pet dogs in Britain in 1917). (*The Bystander*, 30 May 1917)

'Bluffing the Periscope. Taking Cover from U-Boats: Hints for Bathers Necessarily Nervous about Submarines Off Shore.' (*The Sketch*, 27 June 1917)

'When the Raider Drops In – Hints to Householders.' (*The Bystander*, 4 July 1917)

'IF – Adam and Eve had been Germans.' (*The Bystander*, 29 August 1917)

'IF – Noah had been a German!' (*The Bystander*, 29 August 1917)

'Suggestion for Utilising Enemy Trench Mortars Captured in France.' (*The Illustrated Sporting and Dramatic News*, 1 September 1917)

'The Persuading of the Pacifist – Even More Unpleasant Than Swallowing His Own Words.' (*The Bystander*, 5 September 1917)

'The Tank. Mrs. Jones: "What's wrong wi' the dorg, Garg?" Garge: "W'y, the old thief's been an' swallered my War Bonds; so I've got to pay 'im into the bank."' (*The Sketch*, 2 January 1918)

'The Limit! Mrs. Blennernuggit: "Well, now, I *do* call that rude! And so many aeroplanes about, too!"' (*The Bystander*, 2 January 1918)

'Some Shortages and How They Are Dealt With.' (*The Illustrated Sporting and Dramatic News*, 26 January 1918)

'Cat-Moo-Flage. An Intelligent Use of Camouflage for Exposed Positions in the Metropolitan Area.' (*The Sketch*, 30 January 1918)

'Man Power in the Recruitment Office: A Perfectly Impartial Way of Dealing with Doubtful Cases at the Recruitment Office.' (*The Sketch*, 30 January 1918)

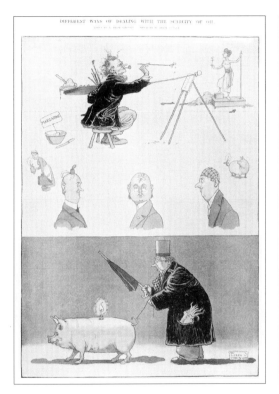

'Different Ways of Dealing with the Scarcity of Oil.' (*The Illustrated Sporting and Dramatic News*, 3 February 1918)

'The Last Man.' A comment by Heath Robinson on the already apparent shortage of potential male spouses caused by the war. (*The Bystander*, 13 February 1918)

The *Knuttboro*
lounge suit
7/6
W.HEATH ROBINSON

The *Pottlethorpe*
morning suit
5/10

The *Dribblingham*
rain-proof coat
4/3

NEW FASHIONS FOR 1918
Designed to meet the shortage in tweeds

'New Fashions for 1918 – Designed to Meet the Shortage in Tweeds.' (*The Bystander*, 13 March 1918)

A SCHEME FOR DOING AWAY WITH THE NECESSITY FOR CLOTHES.

'War-Time Economies – A Scheme for Doing Away with the Necessity for Clothes.'
With shortages, taxation and rationing all making dressing in wartime somewhat
challenging, Heath Robinson presents a suggestion for raising the pavements to neck
level to preserve modesty. (*The Strand*, May 1918)

A SENSIBLE WAY OF DOING WITHOUT
BRACES.

'War-Time Economies – A Sensible Way of Doing Without Braces.' (*The Strand*, May 1918)

TO SAVE YOUR BREATH.
THE PENNY-IN-THE-SLOT MACHINE FOR BLOWING OUT CANDLES.

'War-Time Economies – To Save Your Breath. The Penny-in-the-Slot Machine for Blowing Out Candles.'
(*The Strand*, May 1918)

'Long Jock – Canny Kiltie Camouflage.' (*The Sketch*, 22 May 1918)

'XXX. I – Another Mystery Revealed! An Early Experiment in Aerial Gunnery – Now Illustrated for the First Time.' (*The Sketch*, 14 August 1918)

'America in the Field – The New Mortar for Bridging Chasms.' (1918, reproduced in *My Line of Life*)

The American Suction Tank for drawing the enemy from his dug-out

'America in the Field – The American Suction Tank for Drawing the Enemy from His Dug-Out.' (1918, reproduced in *My Line of Life*)

WHEN GERMANY SURRENDERS HER U-BOATS!

WHY NOT USE THE ENEMY CRAFT FOR PEACEFUL SPORT?—RAMMING RABBITS IN THE BALEARIC ISLANDS!

Drawn by W. Heath Robinson. (Copyrighted in the U.S.A. by the Artist.)

'When Germany Surrenders Her U-Boats! Why Not Use the Enemy Craft for Peaceful Sport? Ramming Rabbits in the Balearic Islands.' (*The Sketch*, 30 October 1918)

'Picked From the Woods – Preparing Seeds for the Raspberry Jam Rations.' (*The Bystander*, 20 November 1918)

'War Inventions – Not Needed Now! Robinson Imagines America in the Field! I. A Device for Training Infantry to Dodge Shells.' (*The Sketch*, 11 December 1918)

American barb trousers
For enabling troops to extricate themselves from wire entanglements

'War Inventions – Not Needed Now! Robinson Imagines America in the Field!
II. Barb-Pants – To Enable Infantry to Get Out of Barbed Wire.' (*The Sketch*,
11 December 1918. This version reproduced in *My Line of Life*)

ROBINSON IMAGINES AMERICA IN THE FIELD! III.— ENEMY OBSERVATION - POSTS REMOVED WITH DESPATCH.

'War Inventions – Not Needed Now! Robinson Imagines America in the Field! III. Enemy Observation-Posts Removed with Despatch.' (*The Sketch*, 18 December 1918)

ROBINSON IMAGINES AMERICA IN THE FIELD! IV.—A MESMERIC BARRAGE
CRUMPLING UP AN ENEMY ATTACK.

'War Inventions – Not Needed Now! Robinson Imagines America in the Field! IV. A
Mesmeric Barrage Crumpling Up an Enemy Attack.' (*The Sketch*, 18 December 1918)

Reconstruction

Temporary reconstruction of a letter-box over the bomb-shattered remains of the old

'Reconstruction – Temporary Reconstruction of a Letter-Box Over the Bomb-Shattered Remains of the Old.' (*The Bystander*, 1 January 1919)

'Reconstruction – Afforestation – A Good Beginning in the Provinces.' A town rather over-compensates for the prolific felling of trees that took place during the war. (*The Bystander*, 8 January 1919)

Reconstruction

UNBULLYING BEEF LEFT OVER FROM THE WAR

'Reconstruction – Unbullying Beef Left Over From the War.' The ubiquitous bully beef is painstakingly reconstructed back into joints of meat. (*The Bystander*, 15 January 1919)

'Reconstruction in the Outer Hebrides – Settling a Scottish Soldier on the Land.'
(*The Bystander*, 22 January 1919)

'A Mere Matter of Form: Distressing Mistake of the Cook Recently Released From a Munition Factory.' (*The Illustrated Sporting and Dramatic News*, 26 January 1919)

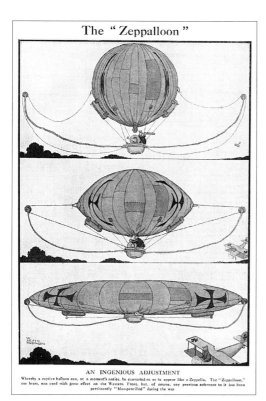

'The "Zeppalloon" – An Ingenious Adjustment. Whereby a captive balloon can, at a moment's notice, be converted so as to appear like a Zeppelin. The "Zeppalloon", one hears, was used with great effect on the Western Front, but, of course, any previous reference to it has been persistently "blue-pencilled" during the war.' The 'blue pencil' was the commonly used term for censorship, so-called because of the colour used in striking out censored information. (*The Bystander*, 29 January 1919)

'Reconstruction in Matrimony – State Encouragement of Marriage for Our Returned Soldiers.' (*The Bystander*, 5 February 1919)

'Reconstruction – Demobilising Our Secret Service.'
(*The Bystander*, 12 February 1919)

'Squaring Trafalgar Square – For "England Expects" –
Anything on Peace Night!' (*The Bystander*, 19 February
1919)

'Hint to the Ministry of Health – A New Fresh Air Bedroom for the Prevention of Flu.' It is estimated that the devastating influenza ('Spanish flu') pandemic in 1918 killed as much as 5 per cent of the world's population. (*The Bystander*, 16 April 1919)

Those Frontiers!

A LITTLE DISAGREEMENT AS TO THE EXACT LINE

The Result Below Stairs

OF UPSTAIRS PERUSAL OF OUR ENTENTE PEACE NUMBER

THE COOK: "'Ow I 'ate these finicky French ways. Gimme old England every time!"

'Those Frontiers! A Little Disagreement as to the Exact Line.' A cartoon representative of the protracted peace negotiations dominating the first half of 1919. (*The Bystander*, 30 April 1919)

'The Result Below Stairs of Upstairs Perusal of our Entente Peace Number. The Cook: "'Ow I 'ate these finicky French ways. Gimme old England every time!"' In June 1919, *The Bystander*, in its own irreverent fashion, celebrated the 'Entente' with France, though this grumpy cook, attempting to cook a frog, does not seem to share the same cosmopolitan spirit as the magazine – or her employers upstairs. (*The Bystander*, 4 June 1919)

'"Peace, Perfect Peace!" Being the Morning After the Night Before.' Peace celebrations did not officially take place until after the signing of the Treaty of Versailles on 28 June 1919. (*The Bystander*, 30 July 1919)

Also available in this series

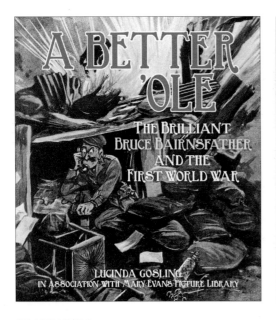

978 0 7509 5595 9

978 0 7509 5597 3